Keltic Creatures Coloring

Kathy O'Meara

Perelandra
Design

This "Keltic Creatures Coloring" Book contains 20 drawings of framed "super-creatures" inspired by figures from the Book of Kells. Coloring these whimsical creatures will provide many pleasurable hours for Children of any age. Each page has 8"x10" guidelines for cutting and framing your finished masterpiece.

Books by Kathy O'Meara

Keltic Crosses Coloring
Keltic Crosses Coloring 2
Keltic Alphabet Coloring: Capital Letters
Keltic Alphabet Coloring: Lower Case Letters
Keltic Coloring: Knots & Numbers
Keltic Coloring: Knotted Nature
Keltic Alphabet Coloring 2: Capital Letters
Keltic Alphabet Coloring 2: Lower Case Letters
Keltic Creatures Coloring
Keltic Creatures For Kids
Keltic Creatures For Kids 2
Keltic Creatures For Kids 3
Keltic Knots For Kids

Stained Glass "Window" Patterns
Spring Flowers
Summer Flowers
Autumn
Circle of Life
Keltic Christian

International Standard Book Number

ISBN-13: 978-1727588750
ISBN-10: 1727588754

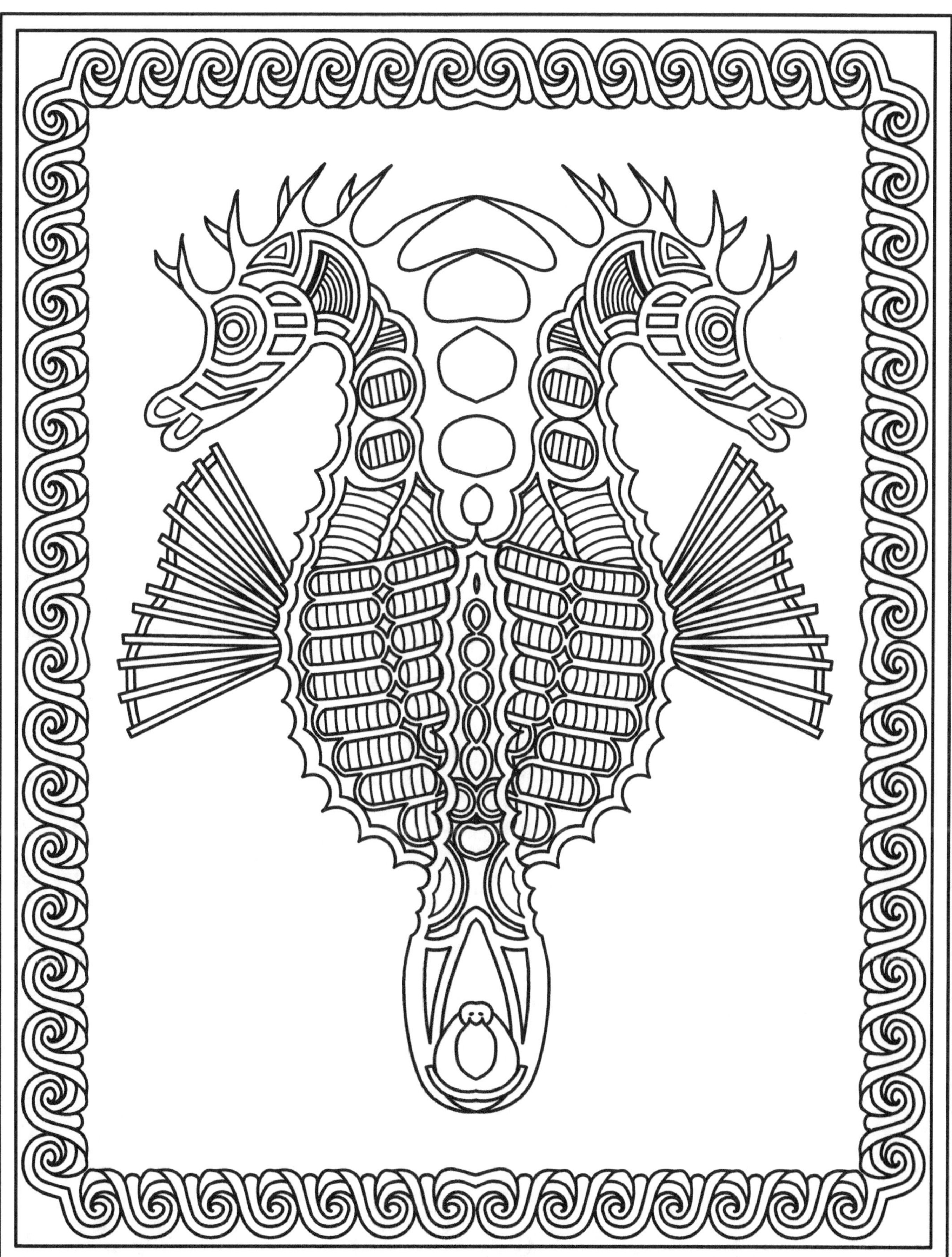